A COLLECTION OF ENGLISH WILD FLOWERS

Produced by the students of Falcon's Academy, an online school, during lockdown 2020

ALEXANDER EWEN

General Editor

Published in 2020 by Michael E Wills

ISBN 978-1-91639-26-8-7 (paperback)

British Library Cataloguing in Publication Data A CIP catalogue record for this book is available from the British Library

www.michaelwills.eu

This book is dedicated to the memory of Ella Thatcher, 2007 – 2018, who is now in another place, but always in our hearts. What fun she would have had looking for the flowers!

A COLLECTION OF ENGLISH WILD FLOWERS

Björn Davies
Finlay Davies
Freja Davies
Alex Ewen
Jessica Ewen
Molly Ewen
Mia Thatcher
Barbro Wills
Michael E Wills

INTRODUCTION

I have been working in the field of education all my adult life. I love teaching and now, though in retirement, the pandemic lockdown has given me a chance to use my somewhat rusty skills to run an online school for my eight wonderful grandchildren.

We started the Falcon's Academy at the end of March, as soon as state schools closed, and have had lessons every weekday at 13.30 on Zoom, until we broke for the summer holiday at the end of July. The lessons have included maths, history, geography, Spanish, (with Chus, our teacher in Salamanca), Swedish and nature studies.

I cannot speak too highly of the students' motivation and effort. This book is just one record of their interests and achievements. It does, however, show how many of us have re-connected with nature during lockdown. The children, (and teachers!) have found, filmed and researched these flowers themselves. One aspect of the study of these plants which we all found fascinating was how many of them, in times gone by, had medicinal uses. All of the flowers were found in South Wiltshire.

Thanks are due to all, but especially to Alex for his work as general editor. With a light touch he standardised the presentations while retaining the character of the children's efforts.

I hope that the thrill of seeing their work in print will be some reward to the contributors for their hard work and that the book will be a lasting memento of our lessons together.

Michael Wills

CONTENTS

Cow Parsley 10
Field Bindweed 12
Marsh Mallow. 14
Cornflower 16
Foxglove 18
Pyramidal Orchid 20
Poppy 22
Common birds-foot trefoil 24
Oregano 26
Ox-Eye Daisy 28
Wild Carrot 30
White Clover 32
Crane's-bill 34
Red Campion 36
Scabious 38
Toad Flax 40
Tansy Ragwort. 42
The Contributors 45

The cover picture is Meadow Crane's-bill

COW PARSLEY

Anthriscus Sylvestris

Other names: Queen Anne's lace

Presented by Alex Ewen

WHAT DOES IT LOOK LIKE/ HOW LARGE CAN IT GROW?

Cow Parsley is a tall plant growing to a metre or more in height.

The umbrella-shaped petals called 'ubels' are typically 3cm to 6cm across. The ubels are in all shapes and sizes.

WHERE DOES IT GROW?

Cow parsley grows in sunny to semi-shaded locations in meadows and at the edges of hedgerows and woodland. It is a particularly common sight by the roadside.

WHAT ARE THE MAIN USES?

The leaves and stems of Cow parsley are reputed to help:

- Anti-inflammatory, antibacterial, antioxidant, antiseptic, antispasmodic problems.
- Coughs, cold and asthma.
- Cancer and epilepsy.

FIELD BINDWEED

Convolvulus Arvensis

Other names: Creeping Jenny

Presented by Jessica Ewen

WHAT DOES IT LOOK LIKE?

It is a trumpet shaped flower with yellow in the middle and white on the outside.

WHERE DOES IT GROW?

Field Bindweed can grow anywhere in gardens or fields. They are very rare in Scotland but usually a common sight in England, Wales and Ireland. It is called a weed but is really a flower growing in the wrong place!

WHAT ARE THE MAIN USES?

Field Bindweed is reputed to be useful for:

- Treating fever
- Urinary tract problems
- Constipation
- Increasing bile production.

MARSH MALLOW

Malva Sylvestris

Other names: Cheese mallow, high mallow

Presented by Molly Ewen

WHAT DOES IT LOOK LIKE/ HOW LARGE CAN IT GROW?

- It can grow to the height of 3 or 4 feet.
- It has heart shaped leaves, which are a bluish greenish colour and covered with hairs on both surfaces.
- They are a violet colour.

WHERE DOES IT GROW?

Marsh Mallow is usually found in Eastern Europe and Northern Africa. It has also recently been seen in North America. The plant is found in marshy (soggy ground) areas or around the sea shores.

WHAT ARE THE MAIN USES?

It is traditionally a herb which is reputed to be useful for:

- Asthma, coughing, throat infections and emphysema.
- Bronchitis and treating wounds or inflammation of the throat, stomach and intestines.

CORNFLOWER

Cyanus

Other names: Bachelor's button

Presented by Michael Wills

WHAT DOES IT LOOK LIKE/ HOW LARGE CAN IT GROW?

The cornflower is a fast-growing, richly blooming herbal flower. It is a wildflower but is often planted in gardens. It has a vividly coloured trumpet shaped bloom.

WHERE DOES IT GROW?

It grows in almost all kinds of environment but prefers arable fields with fertile soil. It got its name because it often grows in corn fields.

WHAT ARE THE MAIN USES?

Dried cornflowers keep their colour and are often used for decoration. When dried, the blooms are edible and can be used in salads. They are also used in Earl Grey Tea!

FUN FACTS

The flower got the nickname Bachelor's Buttons because they were often worn in a buttonhole by boys who were looking for a girlfriend! It is the national flower of Germany and Estonia.

FOXGLOVE

Digitalis

Other names: Goblin gloves, fairy gloves, witches' gloves

Presented by Mia Thatcher

WHAT DOES IT LOOK LIKE/ HOW LARGE CAN IT GROW?

A foxglove is a beautiful flower because of its vibrant colours. You can find them in lots of different colours such as purple, white, pink and a nice rose colour. In every flower there are tiny dots.

WHERE DOES IT GROW?

Foxgloves grow in a whole range of areas including woodland, gardens, moorlands, cliffs and waste grounds.

WHAT ARE THE MAIN USES?

Foxgloves are used for problems such as heart failure and dizziness.

These plants are very poisonous, and it is believed that they are named foxgloves because fairies used the flowers to warn foxes to beware they were being hunted!

PYRAMIDAL ORCHID

Anacamptis Pyramidalis
Presented by Barbro Wills

WHAT DOES IT LOOK LIKE/ HOW LARGE CAN IT GROW?

The shape of this orchid is reflected in its name. It is normally pink but this one is a rare white example. It normally flowers in June and July and has a densely packed flower spike holding up to 100 flowers. It attracts a range of butterflies and moths. This hardy plant reaches on average 10–25 centimetres of height, with a maximum of 60 centimetres. The stem is erect and unbranched.

WHERE DOES IT GROW?

It grows on chalk grassland, coastal habitats, scrub, roadside verges, old quarries and railway embankments. It is native to southwestern Eurasia, from western Europe through the Mediterranean region eastwards to Iran.

WHAT ARE THE MAIN USES?

This flower can be made into Salep (a sticky white substance). It is nutritious and is used in places such as Turkey as an additive in ice cream.

POPPY

Papaverales

Other names: Corn poppy, corn rose

Presented by Finlay Davies

WHAT DOES IT LOOK LIKE/ HOW LARGE CAN IT GROW?

Poppies are short red flowers with black spots in the middle. The vibrant red is used to represent the blood of the people who lost their lives in wars such as WWI and WWII. Although most are short, English poppies can grow up to a metre tall!

WHERE DOES IT GROW?

Poppies can be found anywhere. English poppies are most commonly found in fields, but the Californian alpine poppy can grow on mountains and hills.

WHAT ARE THE MAIN USES?

Poppies were once used as a drug to cure common illnesses. Every year, in November, British people wear these poppies to commemorate those who died during the world wars.

COMMON BIRDS-FOOT TREFOIL

Lotus Corniculatus

Other names: Eggs and bacon, granny's toenails, butter and eggs

Presented by Björn Davies

WHAT DOES IT LOOK LIKE/ HOW LARGE CAN IT GROW?

It is a bright yellow flower that consists of large petals. One of the birds-foot trefoil's other names is eggs and bacon. This is because of its slightly eggy colour and its reddish buds.

WHERE DOES IT GROW?

It is most common in central United States, but it also appears near the south of Canada and in England. It will grow in fields of long grass or even in a swampy area.

WHAT ARE THE MAIN USES?

It is used mainly by bees making nectar for honey. Lots of different species of caterpillars and butterflies feed off this plant making the trefoil important for the survival of these creatures. It also said to help people sleep and calm stomach aches.

OREGANO

Oreganum Vulgare
Other names: ornamental Oregano,
Mexican bush oregano
Presented by Freja Davies

WHAT DOES IT LOOK LIKE/ HOW LARGE CAN IT GROW?

- Oregano is a medium sized plant, its height is 20 -80 centimetres. The plant has thick leaves, 1-4cm long.
- Oregano is a herb and smells and looks a bit like mint to which it is related.

WHERE DOES IT GROW?

Oregano grows in many countries such as:

Cuba, Mexico, England, Sweden and many other European countries.

WHAT ARE THE MAIN USES?

- Oregano is a herb often used in cooking.
- Oil from its leaves has been used against cramp, constipation, diarrhoea and fatigue.

OX-EYE DAISY

Leucanthemum Vulgare

Other names: Moon Daisy, Moon Penny, Marguerite

Presented by Michael Wills

WHAT DOES IT LOOK LIKE/ HOW LARGE CAN IT GROW?

It has large, round flower heads. The flowers are so bright that it is said that they glow in the evenings. The plants can be up 60cm tall and bloom from May until September. The leaves are spoon shaped and jagged.

WHERE DOES IT GROW?

It is very widespread and grows in many kinds of environment, including roadside verges and meadows.

WHAT ARE THE MAIN USES?

The flowers are balsamic and can be made into an infusion for relieving chronic coughs and for bronchial catarrhs.

FUN FACTS

The flower is used for a girl to decide whether her boyfriend is really in love with her. The petals are plucked one after another while saying in turn, “he loves me, he loves me not”. Whichever phrase is said when the last petal is plucked, is the truth!

WILD CARROT

Daucus Carota

Other names: Bees' nest, Bishops lace, Bird's nest

Presented by Björn Davies

WHAT DOES IT LOOK LIKE/ HOW LARGE CAN IT GROW?

It has a mass of tiny white flowers and is easily mistaken for Cow Parsley. Domestic carrots are a variety of this plant. It grows to a height of up to 120 cm and the crown is 30 cm in diameter.

WHERE DOES IT GROW?

It grows along roadsides, meadows and unused fields. It is often considered as a weed and an invasive species which crowds out other wild flowers. Th plant is biennial.

WHAT ARETHE MAIN USES?

Essential oils can be extracted from wild carrot but its main benefit is that it attracts butterflies and insects.

WHITE CLOVER

Trifolium Repens

Other names: Dutch clover, ladino clover

Presented by Jessica Ewen

WHAT DOES IT LOOK LIKE/ HOW LARGE CAN IT GROW?

It is a white flower and it has leaves that normally come in sets of three. The leaf is tear shaped and sometimes has a red stripe across it. They flowers are white and brownish, and they look spiky, but they are not.

WHERE DOES IT GROW?

It grows everywhere, because it is a weed. It grows in fields, gardens, on paths and in meadows. It is native to Europe, North America and Central Asia. It is very common in the United Kingdom as well as on the other side of the globe in New Zealand!

WHAT ARE THE MAIN USES?

The leaves can make tea for colds, coughs and fevers. And the flowers can make tea too!

CRANE'S-BILL

Geranium macrorrhizum
Other names: Meadow geranium, bigroot geranium, geranium pratense
Presented by Barbro Wills

WHAT DOES IT LOOK LIKE/ HOW LARGE CAN IT GROW?

The plant grows in a clump and grows up to a height of roughly 1 m. It is a herbaceous perennial with hairy stems and saucer-shaped blooms of pale violet.

WHERE DOES IT GROW?

The striking bluish-violet flowers of Crane's-bill can be seen in lowland hay meadows, roadside verges and grasslands, particularly ones on chalky soils. Its origins are in the Altai mountains in central Asia.

WHAT ARE THE MAIN USES?

It has been used to cure some diseases such as cholera, dysentery and diarrhoea. It also used to treat nosebleeds and haemorrhoids.

RED CAMPION

Silene Dioica

Other names: Robin hood, adder's flower

Presented by Freja Davies

WHAT DOES IT LOOK LIKE?

Red campions are not actually red but either pink or even purple. They bloom just after the bluebells have gone.

WHERE DOES IT GROW?

Red campions can be found in lightly shaded areas in woodlands, along hedgerows, in fields and ditches and on the side of roads.

WHAT ARE THE MAIN USES?

This plant's seeds were traditionally used to treat snake bite. The root is used as a soap substitute for washing clothes, this is done by putting the root in hot water to get the soap out.

SCABIOUS

Scabiousa
Other names: Pins and needles, pom pom, snake flower, blackamoor's beauty.
Presented by Mia Thatcher

WHAT DOES IT LOOK LIKE/ HOW LARGE CAN IT GROW?

A scabious is usually purple but it can come in white as well. It is called a snake flower because of it's worm like strands. The seeds are on the end of them. It can grow from 30-80 cm tall.

WHERE DOES IT GROW?

These plants can grow in grassland, meadows, grassy verges, hedgerows, river banks and grassy waste ground.

WHAT ARE THE MAIN USES?

Scabious has been used for medicine to treat sore throats and coughing. It is used for your skin complaints such as scabs, eczema, rashes, cracked skin and itching.

FUN FACTS

Scabious is actually a herb!

TOAD FLAX

Linariavulgaris
Other names: butter-and-eggs ,
wild snapdragon and devil's flax
Presented by Finlay Davies

WHAT DOES IT LOOK LIKE/ HOW LARGE CAN IT GROW?

It is a small flower with two shades of yellow. Hence its name "butter and eggs". It is 30 to 80 cms tall and the flower is 2 cm in diameter.

Toad flax is an escaped ornamental flower which was brought to England in the mid-1800's.

WHERE DOES IT GROW?

It is typically found in open, disturbed sites such as roadsides and waste areas or in fields, pastures and edges of forests.

The plant spreads aggressively

WHAT ARETHE MAIN USES?

It was used as a yellow dye for centuries in Germany.

Toad Flax has powerful qualities as a purgative and diuretic and was used for jaundice, liver and skin diseases.

TANSY RAGWORT

Tanacetum vulgare

Other names: Bitter Buttons, Cow Bitter, Golden Buttons.

Presented by Björn Davies

WHAT DOES IT LOOK LIKE/ HOW LARGE CAN IT GROW?

It is a yellow flower with 13 petals and is usually between 20 centimetres to 1 metre tall. There are many flowering heads on the same stalk. The crushed leaves have a very strong smell. The plant is extremely poisonous to many animals including horses.

WHERE DOES IT GROW?

It grows on roadsides, disturbed ground and pastureland where it presents a danger to animals.

DOES IT HAVE ANY MEDICAL OR OTHER USES?

- Ragwort contains poisonous alkaloids which cause the liver to accumulate copper, causing ill heath and death. Although not dangerous to humans, it is toxic for cattle and horses.
- Despite safety concerns, tansy ragwort is used to treat cancer, colic, wounds, and spasms. It is also used as a laxative, to cause sweating, to start menstruation, and for "cleansing and purification."

ANY FUN FACTS?

- Ragwort is important for wildlife as it provides a great deal of nectar for pollinators including a wide range of bees, flies, moths and butterflies.
- It was rated in the top 10 for most nectar production (nectar per unit cover per year) in a UK plants survey.
- It also was the top producer of nectar sugar in another study in Britain.

THE CONTRIBUTORS

ALEX EWEN

20/03/2007

Describe yourself in 3 words:

- Passionate
- Adventurous
- Sporty

I am a passionate football fan. My all-time favourite videogame is Minecraft and I like building football stadiums on the game. My favourite food is olives and my favourite colour switches between red, orange and blue. I go to school at Bishop Wordsworth Grammar school in Salisbury.

DREAM GOAL:

My dream goal is to travel to every country in the world and play football with at least one person in that country (and hopefully win). I would like to be a rich hotel owner who welcomes people from all over the world!

MOLLY EWEN

19/02/2010

Describe yourself in 3 words:

- Cheeky
- Fun
- Caring

I am a passionate worker and love everything. My favourite subject in school is art. I have a guinea pig called Minty and a dog called Digby. I am also looking after ducks called: Percy, Penelope, Fern and June.

DREAM GOAL:

My dream goal is to help save the world from pollution, climate change and to bring peace to the world. My other goal is to be a great dancer, gymnast and to travel the world!

JESSICA EWEN

19/02/2010

Describe yourself in 3 words:

- Loyal
- Fun
- Mischievous

I have a guinea pig called Ivy and a dog called Digby. My favourite colours are orange and blue and my favourite animal is a pig. My favourite sort of food is potatoes! I like it in the countryside because it is more quiet and we get to see more animals. I have got a sister called Molly, we are twins. My brother is called Alex and my parents are called Sarah and Philip.

DREAM GOAL:

My ambition is to help care for the world and become an actor!

FREJA DAVIES

06/10/2009

Describe yourself in 3 words:

- Sporty
- Fun
- Jokey

I like to be active in my spare time, if I am not doing schoolwork. But occasionally, I like to sit down and write a story. The main sport I like is football and the main genre I like to write about is crime. I also like writing diaries and fiction, but now we are in lockdown I have been changing my mind about that. Now I write a lot more non-fiction. During lockdown I have realized that sometimes it is nice to write about things around you and research.

DREAM GOAL:

I want to become a professional footballer or a singer!

BJÖRN DAVIES

05/03/2012

Describe yourself in 3 words:

- Happy
- Kind
- Thoughtful

My favourite sport is football and I like the colour red. I was born in Bath but now I live in Wiltshire. I love the star wars films and I love reading Avatar. I also like television, chocolate biscuits, boomerangs, bikes and cars. What I don't particularly like are eggs and mushrooms – yuck!

DREAM GOAL:

One day I would like to be the avatar!

FINLAY DAVIES

05/03/2012

Describe yourself in 3 words:

- Happy
- Funny
- Sporty

My favourite colour is purple and my favourite sport is race car driving. I was born in Bath but now live in Wiltshire. I love football, cycling, teddies, rugby, cuddling, drawing and reading, but I don't like carrots and broccoli. My favourite film is Paddington Bear and my favourite book is Avatar.

DREAM GOAL:

I want to be the world champion race car driver one day.

MIA THATCHER

26/04/2010

Describe yourself in 3 words:

- Sporty
- Energetic
- Kind

I love to have a laugh with my friends because I am very energetic. My favourite sports are hockey and football. I love spaghetti Bolognese as it is my favourite food. My favourite author is Pamela Butchart and my favourite game is pass the pigs which is a highly addictive pig-rolling game.

DREAM GOAL:

One day I would love to be a world-famous hockey champion!

BARBRO WILLS

03/04/1948

Describe yourself in 3 words:

- Easy-going
- Positive
- Caring

I was born in Sweden but after I was married and had three children, we moved to England in 1979. I had some teaching experience in Sweden teaching English to adults and now I enjoy teaching Swedish to my eight fantastic grandchildren. It makes me incredibly happy to see them embrace their half-Swedish heritage.

www.ingramcontent.com/pod-product-compliance
Ingram Content Group UK Ltd.
Pitfield, Milton Keynes, MK11 3LW, UK
UKHW062300290726
14090UKWH00017B/810